IN THE GRASS

Hoose Colemon 5

IN THE GRASS

HORACE COLEMAN

VIET NAM GENERATION, INC. & BURNING CITIES PRESS

These poems have appeared in the following places:

"A Black Soldier Remembers"—*Between a Rock & a Hard Place*;
    Demilitarized Zones; *From A to Z*; *Radical Visions*
"A Downed Black Pilot Leans How To Fly"—*Demilitarized Zones*; *Giant*
    Talk; *Radical Visions*
"Epiphany #3"—*Incoming*
"In Ca Mau"—*Radical Visions*
"Log: Star Date Now"—*Speak Easy, Speak Free*
"Night Flare Drop, Tan Son Nhut"—*Radical Visions*; *Speak Easy, Speak Free*
"OK Corral East"— *Between a Rock & a Hard Place*; *Itinerary*; *Obsidian*;
    Radical Visions
"Remembrance of Things Past"—*From A to Z*
"War Stories"—*Incoming*

Cover design by Steven Gomes. Woodcut by Cedar Nordbye.

Printed by Viet Nam Generation & Burning Cities Press
18 Center Rd., Woodbridge, CT 06525
email: kalital@minerva.cis.yale.edu
SAN: 298-2412

TO ALL THE WARRIORS
—NO MATTER THEIR AGE, SEX,
NATIONALITY OR
CHOICE OF WEAPON—
IN AND OUT OF UNIFORM.

AND FOR BROOKE, AKEIISA AND DRAKE

AND
ALL THE MIAS
(MISSING IN AMERICA)

CONTENTS

BRING YOUR LUNCH!

"Bring your lunch!" is a phrase from the playgrounds and streets of my youth. You said it to some one you were about to fight. It meant, "I don't know how well you can fight, or who might join in. I don't know if it's going to be unarmed, armed, clean or dirty. But you're going to be at it long enough to get hungry!" All "cultural" warriors need to remember that.

Time is a telescope aimed at your memory and it works like a telescopic washer, sometimes. Things get cleaner and cleaner but mixed up. This is a sorting out.

The Viet Nam war is one of the shapers (distorters) of my age and mind mates. And so much happened in the decade of the Sixties, and its windup and run down, that too much went on for a society, let alone individuals, to easily absorb. The Liberty Bell got cracked again.

Nevertheless, I still rate people by what they reacted to and how they acted and reacted. You could be for or against the war, for instance, and I can respect and understand you and your viewpoint— if you have moral reasons for it. Too many people copped out. Or were indifferent.

Down South, not far from The Redneck Riviera, while in a military "tech school" I went out with some of the guys (white) in my class to have a drink. I must have forgotten what country I was already in. We picked a restaurant and sat down. A Scottish waitress, still on her *real* Green Card, said to our table "I'm sorry but I can't serve the other gentleman." I was "the other gentleman."

There I was with those other young guys, all of us shortly to be "defending" America and "making the world safe for democracy." And I was going to put it all on the line to give some people I've never seen, in a place I'd never heard of until a couple of years ago, what I can't have at home? Nothing new there.

Out with the same guys again, after a week end night of post collegiate heavy drinking, we woke up slightly hung over with rumbling stomachs. We went into the first diner we saw, to eat something—preferably not eggs. The guy who ran the joint charged at us with a meat cleaver, spitting out half-chewed pieces of white bread that made him appear to be foaming at the mouth. Which he probably was. He screamed "Get out! Get out! I ain't having this in here!" Neither did we.

I left Tan Son Nhut, RVN during the middle of the '68 Tet offensive. My self-directed "intelligence," told me we weren't going to win. Complete air superiority aside. Ever hear the GI joke about the best way to end the war? Put all the "good" Vietnamese in a boat and carpet bomb the country from end to end; then sink the boat.

In Sin City (Saigon), where even the rats were tough, a seemingly neverending war—a series of wars, really—and corruption had turned The Pearl of The Orient into a pig pen. I saw poverty, chauvinism, xenophobia, ignorance and money grubbing in all shapes and colors. High/petty officials, cops on the take, hustlers of all kinds (including roundeyes) garnished with ticket punching clerks and colonels who wrote citations for themselves. And the children of war and the hoodlums called "Cowboys." I watched devastation and inflation destroy the efforts, savings and morality of a life time. A bar girl, on a good night, earned a bilingual secretary's monthly salary.

And I saw compassion, courage and bravery, dedication, professionalism, and friendliness when they were in short supply.

During Big Tet my Hammond Flight (the one departing with 101 upright organs) left at night. Tet was some Vietnamese telling America to "Bring your lunch!" The land beneath my departing plane looked like East Dante's Hell. Fifteen seconds of vision condensed decades of war.

Many vets writing poetry about 'Nam use a laconic, stripped down, almost passionless language and a detached point of view. Maybe they're still trying to distance themselves or heighten the

10

impact by saying startling things calmly. "It ain't no big thing. Happens all the time. Besides, you really don't give a damn, anyway. And what you gon' do about it? Send me to Viet Nam?" Maybe it's just style.

Enjoy this book. These poems are reminiscences and folklore. They were written not to please, displease or persuade but to reflect, remind and express. And, no; Viet Nam vets don't just write about the Viet Nam war.

"Get your ass in the grass" means "Do the hard stuff yourself before you tell me how to do it and how to feel about it!" We all have to do that. How? 1) Form a truly good and profound code of conduct and a vision, 2) get educated and trained, 3) get experienced and blooded and, 4) go for the long haul and bring your lunch. America is not through being born and those who do not know history are going to be very damn surprised! And I *still* don't like most civilians. The worst thing is, it's justified.

HC (Parts Two Zero)   17 Nov 94

POEMS

IN CA MAU

In Ca Mau the women
sweep the canal with their oars
on the way to the floating fruit market
bananas
pineapples
grapelets with husks stacked in slender sampans

The Americans in Ca Mau eat tin-skinned food
play prostitute roulette
clap
syph
rigid love with rifles under the bed

The people race bicycles on Sundays
children play soccer on the parade ground
pigs walk the streets alone but
GIs ride 6 to a fast jeep

In the forest of U Minh
500 pound bombs fall 5 miles
and shake the yellow palm-thatched huts
and the yellowed stucco houses
and the yellow tent O Club in Ca Mau

Soldiers hunt communist water buffalo
with quad .50s and infrared
they scream howitzers at suspicious rice
but one bullet
makes a helicopter a shotgunned duck
one rocket trips the man-blind radar
off its legs and the Americans leave
and the women sweep after them

ATTITUDE ADJUSTMENT #2

see what the heads are doing
that the steamers aren't

pick a group

put your bottles and cans
in an ice filled garbage can
or get out the stash, rig, bong
thai sticks, and papers

party until you can
barely stand up or remember
what rank/color/service people are
and the "soldiers" are dead—
again

kill the pain
until the hangover ends
and it's time to do it again
when the war winds down

maybe this one will too—
eventually

JAVA AT 0300

Coffee is for heating C ration cans in
and fishing them out of with a bent coat hanger
shaped like a homemade abortion tool.
You drink it dark as it is outside,
so caffeine and nicotine will
keep you staggering until
it's time to sleep on a desk
for a couple of hours
while hoping the stuff
doesn't eat a hole before
booze and stress corrode your guts.
When Airman Dufuss has figured out
how to make it, we'll have more
when it's the sergeant's color.
You want sugar with that?

LOG: STARDATE NOW

I'm just a lower deck crewman
on Spaceship Earth
(many captains and no navigator).
Our sun is guttering as we scrape the sky
and scratch the face of the God
who watches us go ungently into
a long night. How,
when we've used up all our supplies,
will we use each other, and where,
with what cargo, are we going and why?
My watch is over but the next
helmsman has not reported.
The air from down below
smells of old hunger, angry sweat
and the mutiny I've started.

GOD VISITS ARMAGEDDON

I'm meeting God in the Mekong Delta.
He's waiting till I finish watering
this rice paddy.
Here He comes now,
whirring through the clouds, and
I'm almost done.
He's blowing the dust off.
I can see His plastic nose and
His long green tail. I can feel
His spinning wings hovering
as I'm tossed a dented halo
two sizes too small.

EXILED IN AMERICA

We are the oil,
the precious pressured residue
squeezed out of history.
We are the ones who practice
life astride the knife.
We are numbed by sharp indifference
as the blade turns slowly up.
We are the skinny dreams
that shred fat sleep.
We are the unseen stare raising neck hair,
the wronged, the right.
We are the wind & rain that crack rocks,
the pain that birth unlocks.
We are the oil, soothing
the slow flow of freedom,
moving the earth.
We are.

BLOSSOM TIME

April in Washington is pink and green.
The cherry trees blush beautifully and
the grass grows velvety.
And "dulce et decorum est" to see
our dead in their hallowed holes.

At Arlington our well slain sleep
well groomed as we less brave
honor them in springtime
by walking on their faces.
But we praise our unremembered
and guard our unknowns.

Oh, the dead grow funny flowers
that look like flattened towers.
The common folk sprout small ones
while the generals grow tall ones.

BAD WEATHER FLIGHT

ceiling 300'
visibility 1/4 mile
thunderbumpers

It was a red weather migration
and I was a silver tear
falling out of a cloth grey sky.
I was walking on radar,
a steel star sinking until
finally on beloved but strange soil
I could watch an abandoned moon
pillowed on ragged clouds
and drying in the blackness
I had just left.

WIPING THE AXE

In some African traditions,
the warriors couldn't rejoin life
after taking life,
couldn't come back to the village,
until they had slept with
the first woman they saw.
And she couldn't say "No."
Some groupies,
and/or horny women,
went out to meet the men.
Some lovers (husbands/wives, adulterers)
arranged to meet each other.
The village had to pay for the war
in another way.
The women sacrificed themselves
in another way.
Maybe the old people knew something
we've had to relearn.
Maybe I still need my axe wiped.

A DOWNED BLACK PILOT LEARNS HOW TO FLY

"Now that the war is over,
we'll have to go back
to killing each other.
But, I'll send my medals to Hanoi
and let them make bullets
if they'll ship my leg back.
And, if they mail me an ash tray
made from my F4C,
they can keep the napalm as a bonus.
Next time I'll wait and see
if they've declared war on me—
or just America."

ORIANA FALLACI

It was on a small plane
playing checkers
on the green chessboard of Viet Nam.
Riding with the cargo door open,
swaying in the bumpy air
like drab chandeliers, GI issue,
on our way from Can Tho to Saigon
or was it Saigon to Can Tho?
The loud engines talked
to each of us, alone,
going to, and from, our private hells.
Fallaci, as usual, is beautiful in
braids, unlabeled non-issue fatigues, and loafers.
No story here; no flirtations; no interviews.
Just the quiet of grunts,
a round-eyed woman,
and the danger, somewhere,
we all love.
Now breast cancer may kill her
if smoking cigarettes while
breathing pure oxygen doesn't.
Something is going to
get us all, eventually.

THIS LITTLE PIGGY

This little piggy went to war
& this little piggy tried to score.
This puzzled piggy tried to run
& this foolish piggy was given a gun.
The cool little piggy stayed home & had fun.
And the sad little piggy was wasted and had none.
And this little piggy went all the way
but when he got home it was hard to stay.

TU DO TALK

Now you fini Viet Nam, GI,
where you get steam job and blow bath?
Beaucoup dead go home.
All wounded number one OK now.
Taxi girl nice again; taxi driver
no some more rich and
dinky dao American go
dinky dao America.
Shrinking bird disease stop.
Saigon Cowboys all go Ho Chi Minh City.
Number ten war stop—
number new war begin.
Beaucoup kilos of kilos,
beaucoup people,
beaucoup gone.
What you do now, GI?
You say "xin loi!" Xin loi?
Sorry about that;
sorry about that.
You fini Viet Nam,
Viet Nam fini you.
Maybe your street without joy
paved with shit—
maybe road to bitterness.

THE PROVINCIAL POET COMES TO TOWN

for Mao

riot in the street shakes the city
the rumble from the country sweeps the land
do not ask who I am
strangers will tell you

NIGHT FLARE DROP, TAN SON NHUT

It is Tet (some Vietnamese excuse for fireworks)
and the war sneaks into Saigon
while young girls from villages in the Delta
who have learned to use make up and read comic books
suck off fat Air Force colonels.
All is joy.

Roman candles chase tracers;
little rockets bark at dancing dragons.
In the foreign cemetery at the entrance to the base,
dying soldiers are having a colorful fire fight.
Six Vietnamese MPs, eager to watch,
run into a mine field and throw yellow confetti for yards.
In 100 P Alley boy pimps laugh and sell
three-day-old sandwiches to Americans
afraid to come out of their rooms.

No chauffeur driven Mercedes,
for the first time in years,
bull through the streets.
Trapped in the bar at The Tomb
(Tan Son Nhut Officers Open Mess)
off-duty pilots in dirty flight suits
stand in front of the air conditioners
sweating.

Overhead frightened planes circle,
shedding magnesium tears
that burn deep holes in the night.
But the dark, like the VC,
always comes back.

WAR STORIES

I don't know any war stories.
I could tell you about
the good old boy sergeant
who liked to ride with the
forward air controllers in light planes
and shoot water buffalo and kids
or the VC province chief
posing posthumously for pictures
or the ARVN who lost his arm to the NVA,
his wife to a free fire zone,
and his kid to disease and
American medicine
and the street whores I'd let in
to hide from the "white mice"
(Vietnamese cops)
when I was den dad
opposite Soul Alley
or the Saigon rats who'd stop foraging
in the street long enough to stare me down
but I don't know any war stories
except for the cracker pilot
who was ashamed to say "thanks"
when I rescued him.

HIS EYE IS ON THE SPARROW

I sent my parents,
not so long ago it seems,
a picture of the little bird
with twine wrapped around its leg
that had burst his heart
in the struggle
to free itself when
the string's free end
had caught in some barbed wire.
I wrote on the picture's back
"Now I know what it means
when they say,
His eye is on the sparrow."
Things change.

A BLACK SOLDIER REMEMBERS:

My Saigon Daughter I saw only once,
standing in the dusty square across
from the Brink BOQ/PX, in back of
the National Assembly, not far from the
ugly statue of the crouching marines facing
the fish pond the VC blew up during Tet.

The amputee beggars watch us.
The girl and I have the same color
and the same eyes.
She does not offer me one of
the silly hats she offers Americans
but I'm not Senegalese and
I have nothing she needs but
the sad smile she already has.

AND THEN HE SAID

"The world runs best when America runs it!"
Not that he ever intends to change the oil—
or even pay for the gas.
He just thinks he'll drive right past the toll booth,
through the crowd, over the curb, and park in a
nice close-in handicapped spot right by the door.
Because he can get the tickets fixed and
a new blonde every year.
And he will.

Until one drunken rainy night,
when his credit is no good,
his license is revoked,
and the lease is expired.
The Repo Man's gonna haul it
all away and leave him
dancing with the semis
in six lanes of fast death.

THE WALL

This simple place
etched with graffiti
naming the dead
was designed by the daughter of
a woman I know
who tried with her husband
to keep their child safe
from political opinions and controversy
not knowing the young woman
would be the architect
of hatred
frustration
envy

and a healing blackness

THE ADRENALINE JUNKIE AND
"THE DAILY EMERGENCY"

Once my heart actually stops at Tan Son Nhut as
(the world's busiest airport then where
a radar screen looks like bagless popcorn
puffing up behind a microwave's glass door)
I just see a dot streaking toward four F4Cs I'm "controlling"
so I snap out the flight leader's call sign saying "Traffic, 12 o'clock,
5 miles, closing fast!" and the pilot grunts "Pull up, fast!" as he pulls Gs
and I wonder if you can hear a midair through a closed mike
but I only hear "Thanks" (so I know it's close).
And then there's monsoon when it rains sideways and
the VC love to play and some dingbat calls (brags about) "Bingo Fuel!"
and wants an *immediate* hand-off to RAPCON with a straight-in approach
(meaning he's going to flame out and crash in five minutes)
so I say, coolly, because that's the only way, "Roger, you're third,"
and he says "No, *you* don't understand, *Bingo* Fuel!" so I say "Squawk
flash," then "Radar contact, you're *third!*" and add
(so he knows what the score is), "The flight in front of you has three
and the flight in front of *it* has two minutes," meaning
"Don't bug me with the small stuff—let me work,"
or it could be the perfect rescue when I've got top cover over the crash
and choppers on the way but the guy is so low his 'chute doesn't open and
it's body bag time or the jet jockey gets shot down and I'm
trying to get a fix on him so I can tell the chopper where to go—
I *know* where the chopper can go—
and I say, "Look, stay in one place so I can steer these guys in,"
and he breathlessly says, "They're chasing me," and I give him a zipper
(two mike clicks in acknowledgment)
because there's nothing to say, or a pilot from Thailand is late for
an awards ceremony and can't wait to be worked through the traffic so he
leaves my frequency to crack up close to Bien Hoa, winning a new piece
of tin for his tomb, and they want to court martial *me* because if there's a

dead pilot and a live controller, guess who's guilty?— until the tapes save
my ass—or how about the guy pinned under the skid of a Huey with a
dead engine and I can't find a Chinook to get the damn thing off him
before he's pushed face down into the mud so Hueys keep landing and
their crews muscle the thing off him—wonder if he made it?— and *another*
F102 has *another* AC/DC power failure and some guy comes back with his
instruments out and the canopy blown and every piece of dirt and paper
that ever was in that bird is blinding him, swirling around the cockpit at
Mach .5 at least as I try to make an intercept with a chase plane so it can
match speeds and get him down mostly in one piece, or B52s are going to
drop some fresh-from-Guam bombs
on an Army field headquarters and SAC doesn't talk to peons
and I've seen two out of three kids born—a real rush—and sex is nice too,
booze, going too fast and some drugs
but there's nothing like trying to get a chopper load of guns and ammo
to the American Embassy during Tet while the VC are downstairs blowing
doors and grunts are throwing hand guns through the windows to civilians
racing to the roof and I'm giving directions to
a chopper from the boonies with an old street map
assisted by a Saigonese sergeant (who only speaks
broken English and my Vietnamese isn't too tough)
and I can't even see the bird on radar he's so close but
he finally finds the place—and gets shot down and I wonder
"Who's got the guns now? Who's hurt or hit?" and I say to myself
"Well, this is *another* fine mess you've gotten us into."

CRACKS IN THE WALL

It's not even symbolic—
The Wall has "structural weaknesses"
(lines of stress in its facade).
Why should the monument
be less flawed, more soundly made,
than the war, the country's feelings,
individual opinions or
the warriors' reception?
Maybe all those tears eroded it.
Something's been undermined.
I got cracks in my walls and
I won't even tell you
where they were made.
Puller's kid could have said
"The war's not over
until the last suicide."
We know we built
as good as we could.
What's wrong with
a stone Liberty Bell?

SHAKA ZULU

"The object of war is not to die for your country;
it's to get the other poor son of a bitch to die for his!"
General George "Reincarnated" Patton supposedly said.
And his Colonel son allowed as how
"I do like to see the arms and legs fly!"

They should have met the beetle that burrowed
a whole new way of death. This Zulu kid invented
new weapons, new tactics, new training
and a mood to match them.
Like killing his own infant son to avoid
the distractions of a fight for succession.

What can I say? The guy had his priorities straight.
You got to bring ass to get ass and you
can't be looking over your shoulder
all the time while you're making
unwilling people into more than
they can be.

He rewarded those who could, who ever they were,
listened when he should, shut them up when
they rambled and cut the crap of religion out of the tribe.
"Leave no living enemy behind!" was his creed.
And he was first to let his thirsty spear drink.

He built a machine to build an empire
and devoted an empire to maintaining
his ruthless, vicious, victorious killing machine.
So, he conquered all but his weaknesses
and excesses. And his own people
were safe from everything but him.
His frightened, jealous kin and tribesmen
killed him. And rode his machine,
but not as well as he, of course.
Can you wonder why I love him so?

THE CONQUEROR

"*For an assassin there are no crimes . . .*
that is, of course, if he thinks clearly."
—Malraux, *The Conquerors*

that shadow in the night is Ch'en
the wingless angel who practices death
who hugs killing like a wound sucks steel
into its oozing mouth

Ch'en in the dead man's bedroom
looks at him beneath his mosquito net
safe as an Arab woman behind her veil

and Ch'en
at the end of habit
slowly stabs the flesh of his own arm
needing to know his knife truly
before the bed springs fling
the body up and he must
hold the sawing blade in

both men shudder
as Ch'en joins Cain's clan
and flees skillfully as
what's worth killing for
is worth living through

I DON'T SUPPOSE I'LL EVER FORGET

The guy in the Vet Center who started dreaming
about those dark hootches he used to
crawl into and out of and cut throats.
He still gets visits from the Secret Service
when the President passes through town.
And peoples' old ladies kept having "mystery" babies.
Or they'd get the divorce papers after she'd moved,
sold the house, and bought a new car.
The parties where everybody brought a fifth or
a case and nobody left till all the "soldiers" were dead.
Ol' Bear wanting to shoot the lieutenant
(which wasn't a bad idea but he was too nice a kid to
have to do the time) so I took it away from him.
Then there was the night they brought the VC in
(labor detail on their way to the Chieu Hoi Center for some R&R)
and nobody told us they were coming so the bolts going back
on the 16s sounded like a cricket convention
as I scoped the little skinny fuckers out real good
and not one came up to my shoulder or had any real meat.
I could have punched them all out real easy; they looked
just like the hired help but unafraid so I just kept
watching me watching them until one laughed
and put a "V" of fingers and then a thumb and forefinger
to his mouth so I tossed them a canteen and some "Say-Lems"
and we all smoked and I didn't even ask for the pack back.

YOU CAN'T TELL THE PLAYERS
WITHOUT A SCORECARD

Especially after the colonel's secretary put a
bomb in the spook shop and blew it up
I wondered if I knew any of the sappers who played us for saps Easter
Sunday when the VC had rested long enough
and broke into, and out of, the Chieu Hoi camp,
after cutting the head off the mayor's daughter and doing same same to his
arm, burned the town and shot a few people for luck.
How, the morning Tet started
Beau Coup Kilo and I were having breakfast in the O Club
after the usual 14-hour night shift and bouncing champagne corks off the
ceiling to celebrate the New Year's and Christmas we hadn't had when the
PA told all personnel to report to their units to help fighters drop bombs at
the end of the runway and APs shot up our radar and some
kid airman trying to help waste VC and steered a chopper full of ammo
and weapons over to the guys getting killed at the embassy so the VC
could blow it out of the air and resupply themselves and then we had to
guide some Cobras to Cholon so they could kill some ARVN generals
'cause they all look alike from the air. That was after the 52s were going to
drop on that Army field headquarters and some paper pusher got a Silver
Star after *I* stopped them which was OK with me since I didn't want our
CO touching me since he wouldn't even give us weapons during Tet—
"Turn out the lights! They won't see you!"—and when I got home after
the Detroit riots I had been away so long that when I went into the
drugstore Saturday morning and asked "What was all the shooting last
night?" they just look at me with
Vietnamese eyes and I *don't* know any war stories—
except for the fool in the ambush who
shouted: "Come on, you guys! Ain't no little
yellow sonofabitches gonna keep *me* pinned down!"
and jumped up and got one right between the eyes.
Now *that's* funny.

D-DAY + 50; TET + 25

It's been all my life since Normandy
and half my life since Tet.
And the scars my father and I
share in our minds are half-healed.
The shock of survival can be
worse than other wounds.
We didn't know there would be
seams on our souls.
Maybe the next time
the daughters get to go.
It's not just brittle men who
wake up wet and screaming,
tangled in new sheets and old situations.
It seems, Galileo not withstanding,
damn near everyone reaches the heights—
and the depths—at the same time.
But we'd still do it again, even if we know
the stories before their 10th syllable
or the second spilled drink
at the VA, Legion Hall, AMVETS,
Vet Centers, VFW, parks,
parking lots or at The Wall.
It beats being bored.

Z-GRAM

One quarter century later,
Admiral Zumwalt returns to Viet Nam
(still speaking "no talk" well).
"To come in and meet with people
who were adversaries for so long
on policy issues of mutual interest
is really an exciting experience."

He met with General Vo Nguyen Giap
who made no gap in Z's heart,
though he was an old foe.
The thing that ate Elmo Zumwalt III
(and cracked the grandson's egg) did.
The Admiral's kid died in the war
but didn't fall there.

"I operated in areas so heavily hit
with Agent Orange they looked like
burned-out World War II forests," said III
before reporting to oblivion's billet.

"He was almost certainly alive,"
the Admiral believes—or at least said—
"as the result of the use of Agent Orange
and the great reduction in casualties
that stemmed from defoliation."

"I would use Agent Orange again today
in similar circumstances if
we didn't have noncarcinogenic defoliants,
because we greatly reduced
the deaths and wounding."

Agent Orange said nothing,
working silently and thoroughly,
slowly reducing truth
and defoliating people.

While Admiral Z is still
talking to himself

THE WORST JOB IN THE AIR FORCE

I drive the valiant blue Valiant
to the bereft and bereave them.
I say:

Dear Sir or Madam or Mrs,
it is my sad duty to inform you that
your husband, son, brother, father (choice of one)
is dead/missing in action/marrying a Vietnamese
and beloved by all his comrades and commanders.

(A. Ground) While on a sweep of the
Central Highlands, Saigon bars, DMZ
he threw himself on a whore/grenade/1st Lt.
thereby sparing his comrades or

(B. Air) Flying from the MPs, Thailand, Phu Cat
he machine gunned/took pictures of/sprayed
16 of the little bastards before they
got his young ass, rendering vital service
before he was rent.

The body, head, or other remains may be sent to the
local undertaker of your choice or
viewed at the nearest military installation
with his rank embroidered upon them.

Gratuities
          are not necessary

THE TOUCH

the touch of death
thrills like some
unfamiliar hand
between your legs
vivid as
remembered lightning
striking vaguely but
is nothing to fear
till that last quick visit

REMEMBRANCE OF THINGS PAST

mortars are the devil coughing
napalm?
Baudelaire never had such flowers
such bright fleur de lis
such evil

claymores
shatter more than bones

when they attacked we
killed them dreams and all
we thought

we fire artillery they
shot hatred back

when we burned their bones
they loathed us still dying
still trying to get their crisp
fingers on our throats

THE PLOT TO ASSASSINATE
THE STATUE OF LIBERTY

They were delinquents—acting too late.
Going after the old whore like brave young vandals,
acting the way you do when you're scared and angry, breaking
something no one will miss.

And she was always standing there
where they could see her.
Needing deodorant under at least one arm.
Doing as much harm as stinking could,
as much good as prayer would.
And wearing herself out just standing there,
wearing the same moldy green dress day after day.
And just standing there,
flaunting her diseased, contagious self—
ruined by that social illness of hers.

So, why not go over to Liberty's Island
(they put her there to keep it from spreading);
why not go over there and blind her like justice is,
rob her like hope does?

What could she do but
whine what all failures mumble:

> I should have been something.
> I should have been something that meant something.
> I should have stood for something.

And not just stood there,
in that crappy dress,
looking like a big tired turd,
acting like she didn't know everybody
has to flush their own shit.

You wonder why anybody would have ever
paid good money for her or bothered to try
to bash her head in. Dumb kids,
stealing an empty purse.
She never had nothing no way.
Dumb kids, trying to kill a corpse.

NOTES FOR VETERAN'S WAR PROTEST

Ralph: concerning plans for the local march,
the following:

1. Saw the weary demonstration in Washington,
the burning faces of our sad boy warriors
throwing their medals over the White House fence.

2. Think we should emulate but not copy, so:
when the delegation arrives at the state capitol
first read the petition:

> "We are not afraid to kill. We are sorry we
> murdered our souls. We did as told but we learned how to
> say NO! Stop it. Or we will stop you. Don't resist. You
> can't stop the ghosts you made of us."

3. Next, have those who lost legs crawl forward and neatly stack
them. Then bowl the skull of your best killed buddy down the
aisle.

4. Finally, have the blind push the quadriplegics forward. They
 will have knives in their teeth to give to the legislators to use on
themselves. We leave. If they don't use them we come back.

Horace

PS. Save the instructions for your grandkids. They'll come in
handy.— hc

THE RAID NEAR SAIGON

Sitting before the height-finder radar
we see the blip/shapes of unseen bombers
miles high and away.

Thick as mosquito eggs
on the circled surface of a pond,
bombs drift like dying fireflies,
like murderous ghosts
falling in green streaks.

At the bottom of the screen,
electronic dust spills upward
and before we can speak,
the floor rumbles.

OK CORRAL EAST

Brothers in The Nam

Sgt Christopher and I are in Khanh Hoi,
down by the docks in the Blues Bar.
The women are brown and there is no "Saigon Tea."
We're making our nightly HIT ('Hore Inspection Tour),
watching the black inside and out, digging night sights,
soul sounds and getting tight.

The grunts in the corner raise undisturbed hell
as the timid MP's freckles pale.
He walks past the dude high in the doorway,
in his lavender jump suit, to ask the mamma-san,
quietly, about curfew.

He chokes on the weed smoke as
he sees nothing his color here and
he fingers his army rosary—his .45.

But this is not Cleveland or Chicago;
he makes no one here cringe and
our gazes, like punji stakes, impale him.

We have all killed something recently,
know who owns the night,
and carry darkness with us.

STILL LIFE WITH DEAD HIPPIE

It's all in the point of view.
Suppose you have your
sophored out sophomore
slumped on the sidewalk
in the foreground.
Never made it to the bar.
His buddy's embarrassed
& his girl is outraged.
No fun tonight, Hon!

Or, maybe there's this
feminist witch exercising
her anger on this
newly stricken MCP
while the stunned bastard
in bell-bottoms looks for reasons.

It could be a pink-faced VC broad
trying to grasp the life that's
just flown from your
unfavorite dumb son. And
she has no right to cry out
in plain sight, to be so
full of pain. You have to
blame her for
the cluck's bad luck.

Of course, what it was,
was these dirty, rotten,
vicious whore kids—
standing around watching
the overarmed, undertrained
National Guard about to go wild.

And, yeah, those kids were fools,
some of them, believing in democracy
and free speech and other book stuff
as if it belonged in the real world.
Out there chucking rocks & slogans & curses.
Full of dope, sex, & unAmerican
antiwar ideas. They were coming
out of class, out of their stupor,
sitting on & smoking grass.
Reminding *you* that
something's wrong & some one has
to do something. So, it's *their* fault
that it's not their fault!

Then we find out
there were no snipers
or syphilitic commie call girls
recruiting on campus &
that girl was just
a terrified runaway barely
old enough to bleed but
just the right age to
understand the deed.

And did you ever notice
how that cheap statue
down there in Columbus
of the used car salesman
toting forged registrations
past the Capitol building
looks just like Governor Rhodes?

PEOPLE'S WAR, PEOPLE'S ARMY

It used to be the king who rode in front and
charged first to bear the brunt of them.
Armored brightly, his priest-blessed sword
whistling lightly through the air—
a manly, lordly, Lord.

Then the knights thundered out on heavy horses
whose hooves struck sparks and sundered stones.
The archers darkened the sun and
we cheered their arrows home.

Man to man, we on foot fought through the town.
Fang, fair, or foul it went.
Hand up or knife down.

The peasants crept to the castle
with their families and their all
to stand the sieges with sorrow.
No better when we win,
slaughtered when we fall.

Now, show me a leader
with a weapon in his hand
as they chess us about
from land to land.

"For love of the lord," spake the bishop.
"Strike this hour," quoth the chancellor.
"Take the power" said the scholar.
"Gold and glory" sang the barons.

Lad, don't listen when their lies ring
and kill for the love of the thing.

COSMOLOGY, SURVIVAL AND VIET NAM

Seat mates on a plane

So this guy says "The universe is boxed in time
and wrapped with energy.
But snakelike waves of gravity,
expansions, and contractions move through
what on the way to where? All I know is
progress doesn't end,
though where it leads is uncertain.
Maybe reality is a local option?
Maybe entropy is part of creation?"

And I said
"What I need you can't get at the store.
I got 7 holes in my face that get filled
with sweat, tears, mucous, blood
and someone else's lips if I'm lucky.
so I better get over it because
everybody's got their list of lies,
loves and loses and
some scars don't show."

NIGHT CANVAS

Sometimes I go outside
and watch the flame tailed
reconnaissance birds—
blue/orange jet pencils
writing on a black sky—
when Viet Nam was beautiful
and I hoped all the good guys
came back alive that time.

EPIPHANY #3

One day, riding a bus with
mesh covered windows from
Tan Son Nhut to Saigon,
I heard two green grunts
so arrogantly loud that
I couldn't help eavesdropping:
"These people are really dumb—
they don't even speak English!"
That's when I knew America
would never win this war.

EXCERPTS FROM A MERCENARY'S DIARY

Never deny reality,
overlook the obvious
or BS yourself.
Take three—one to use,
one to lose and one to break.
Admit you're doing it because
someone wants it done.
Believe something—even if
you have to make it up.
Do good work.
Have something
more important
than you,
worth dying for, and
worth living for.
Look out for your buddies
and your men.
Pay your debts.
Keep your word and
don't use too many of them.
Don't take too much shit
from any one.
Pay your enemies back.
Smile sometimes and
laugh when you can.

THE RIFLE IN THE RACK

I guess I should have known
  when I told wife #1 I didn't want
  to meet new neighbors (and
  that was *before* Nam) because
  I didn't need to know any bodies
I guess I should have known
  that night in bed when
  I wrapped my arms around
    an AR-15 instead of Simone
  or years later when wife #2
  told the kids, "Daddy doesn't like airplanes"
   and the look on my face
   spoke what I couldn't
I guess I should have known
  when the boy said, "How come
   Daddy's so mean?"
I guess I should have known
  when the girl flinched when I touched her
And I guess *you* should know
—you don't want to get me mad
—I *still* don't like civilians
—it has to come out some way
—wiping out a bunch of strangers
in McDonald's won't do it and
I'm looking for just one woman
(if I could let her touch me)
to thaw out with

BEEN THERE, DONE THAT

war
marriage
(2 more wars)
children
(3 known)
hired
fired
laid off
and there sure have been
a lot of people at parties I've paid for

HOME FRONT/PCOD

I

Sell the house and buy a car?
Or, buy a house and sell the car?
Take the kids and move.
Fire the husband/lover
(taking the last three checks)
or get a new lover/husband?
Have a baby two weeks
after The Old Man gets home or
be pregnant when he gets there.
Start an affair or add another guy
to the string of ones screwed on a hood
behind the NCO Club. But then a woman
needs a man like a fish needs a bicycle.
I guess we were all dancing in Shiva's fire
when we were soldiers once so young.

II

You better use your dick today.
You might not be able to—
or have one—tomorrow.
Anyway, your wife is moving as fast
with her legs in the air
as she does on her feet.
Needs first, convention last
in the new (old) morality.
And in a church or in an alley,
I know the price of a woman.
If she costs more, she's a wife.
But like my cuz says, "It's not about
beating the knees," and who knows
how the next war or woman is
going to turn out?

III

You ever piss green paste?
That's one way to miss your PCOD
(pussy cutoff date)
when the whores don't like rubbers.
You could try for that Viet Nam Rose
that makes you look like
you're always blushing or go until
you get The Black Syph that
gets you an all-expenses-paid trip
to No Name Island with the others
who crapped out in sexual roulette or
be like Airman X and have
"nonspecific ureathritis" 3 times so
he could see if fate still works
within established parameters.
Is all "love" guilty or
are "professional lovers"
better than amateurs?

TO A YOUNG GUY I KNOW IN SOMALIA

Yeah, you want to know
if you can do what you gotta do
when you gotta do it.
Your single mother did a long time ago.
When there's incoming,
you might drop everything
below the waist.
Don't get embarrassed if you get wet.
You'll learn to pucker.
Just don't end up
wearing a T-shirt that says
SOMALIAN WAR GAMES—SECOND PLACE.
They've already told you:
Don't drink the water!
Don't eat the food!
Don't screw the women!
You always do—and pay for it,
some kind of way.
Do what you gotta do
to live with staying alive.
Ain't nobody in that foxhole with you
but maybe a guy whose name
you might not remember next month.
Hope you make it back.
I'll buy you a drink anyway.

GI GENIUSES

"We all get blooded different ways but
civilians don't know like GIs do.
So when I've got on
an old T-shirt saying
'Second Place' on the front and
'Southeast Asian War Games' on the back,
duck.'"

"Spilling brains is just
another kind of orgasm.
Once you're used to
a dirty soul
a brass tongue
fear stink
wet hands
and shriveled balls
you get to liking them—
until the rush wears off
and you need another fix
to turn off your mind movies."

"I like the
imitation travel poster that says
'Travel to exotic lands—
meet strange people—
and kill them'"!

"Having the kids whine,
the wife nag or
the boss chew you out
doesn't mean much
after you've fragged your first officer."

"Besides 'back in the world,'
'it don't mean nothing,' and
'What you gonna do?
Send me to Viet Nam?'
the thing I like best goes
'This is where the unwilling
are made to do the unnecessary
by the unqualified
for the ungrateful,'
'cause that sums up Nam,
marriage, religion, work,
this country and life. See?

THE DUFFEL BAG

Everything I own
that's really important,
is mostly olive drab and fits
in a duffel bag, my hands,
around my waist
or on my shoulders.
There's another set of fatigues,
socks, soap, underwear,
personal piece, shaving cream,
a couple of magazines—
not the reading kind and
not taped into an imitation super-long,
double-ended banana clip;
they bend that way—
gun oil, two paperback books
(neither one a Bible),
pictures of stateside people
and in country friends and places,
a travel clock-radio,
medical and pay records, orders,
hair brush, toothbrush, razor,
insect repellent, a bayonet, an M16
and a guitar.

after all this time
everything fits except
the olive drab feelings
I still have

WHAT IT WAS

Finding out almost more than I can stand
about me and others in smelly fatigues
or clean civvies

Respecting nothing and no one

A dress rehearsal for living

More practice in quickly judging
the value of a woman
the price of a man
the worth of a child

How uncivilized the
seemingly sophisticated are

The proper attitude for an extra
in Kipling's *Tommy Atkins* poems

Licking honey off barbed wire

Surveying the borders of cowardice and courage
while mapping love and fear
and ignorance and arrogance

Making a sturdy existential shipping carton
packed with slippery political nothing

Power full of impotence

Being washed down a fast river
full of slippery jagged rocks
while drinking off a battered coffin

Learning Einstein is wrong
about God and shaved dice

Seeing night fire fights announce bomb drops so
exploding bodies and artillery can make
new holes in the earth while parachute flares
are dangling white commas on a page
black as Dante's hell

SAIGON WARRIOR

So my fatigues don't get muddy or bloody or even
too sweaty (the air conditioning's for the equipment—not me).

That doesn't mean I don't fight my necessary way
or feel for the grunts or get shot at in the streets.

Or that I don't feel disgusted the one time I go
to the Caravelle Hotel (where they still make
table cloths and flatware and the Vietnamese imitation of
a rock band isn't bad after the third gin and tonic) until
I look out over the river, see tracers and know
they're dying out there.

I figure you could have two lines—like a weekend showing at
a theater with popular movies—and one would be
those I've helped kill and one those I've helped save
and there might be more women, children and old people in one
but they can take you out of here too and some one else is going to
have to see if all the napalm and white phosphorous that make
"Crispy Critters" or turn flesh into puddles and cluster bomb units
(like round aerial shotguns loaded with plastic buckshot that
don't show up on X-rays) or simple high explosives, ground or
air bursts (or jettisoned fuel tanks that hit Co Nguyen in the head
while she's fixing dinner) and the ghosts they made equal
the living bones from the times I played junior guardian angel.

So now it's time to go to The Wall and say "Hello" or
look a Vietnamese in the face and smile and
some one else can see which way my scale tilts.

IT WAS JANE FONDA'S FAULT!

or *College, Again*

Stirring us up.
Looking good.
Making sense.
Too many of us had
weirdly & recently
seen people buy it.
Tim Butz
(of later *Counterspy* fame)
came by a day or so afterwards.
Organized and left.
Doing it again
some place else
Fonda went.

When we reached our assembly point,
people used old habits to pick leaders
(date of rank).
The little I had was enough.
So I led 'em out singing:
"*And it's one, two, three,
what are we fighting for?*"
And we really *knew* this time,
straggling toward a building
I sat in.

After we searched and destroyed
some "Vietnamese villagers"
right in the middle of ROTC's
new tin soldier party,
we talked to the crowd.
A smug kid student
(must have had a
high draft number
and a low "reality IQ")
thought he'd shut me up by saying,
"Well, you must know; you've been there."
I splattered his face with,
"Try thinking for your self,
instead of believing
whoever yells loudest!"
then bounced a Bronze Star ribbon
off a colonel so conditioned
he almost returned
the knife sharp salute
I gave him as we left.

FLASH FORWARD

FLASH

(ode to "civilians")

Well, I finally had that dream.
You know, the silent
vividly colored
real slow motion one
where you watch yourself
be part of The Way Wild Bunch?
I've got new fatigues
(already spotted with potent perfume):
0800 sweat, gun oil, dried blood,
human manure (from rice paddies),
rotten fish sauce that had
oozed down a hot runway
and onto me
(like someone getting "spilled").
Fear-stink and eau de cordite
wrinkle noses on dead faces
whiffing themselves
as if it was whiskey.
A toke from a Thai stick, maybe,
a "shotgun" from a shotgun
or a brew could clear all that up
—for a New York minute.
And I'm hitting everything I'm aiming at.
The Mattel Shoot 'N' Shell
doesn't need a thumb extractor today.
The fighters are *almost* on target and
the LT *almost* read the map right.
Like we *almost* have
the right strategy (and politics).
Not that it really makes any difference.
I'm wasting *every* one—reticent men,
defiant women, resigned old people,
semi-innocent children.
And, all the "slopes," "dinks" and "zips"
have round eyes.

FORWARD

(ode to "civilians")

Especially the burning coed who says,
in her California accent,
"How come you Vietnam vets
are *so* crazy?" So I tell her
"Because people like you
ask questions like that!"
Then I give her half a magazine
to read with her half a mind
until she has half a body.

Now I don't worry about going to sleep
(and waking up in pieces or not at all
or just waking up),
blowing my warm cool and
killing someone accidentally
instead of on purpose.
One piece of peace cures
a lot when I finally admit
who and what
the *real* "enemy" is:

The grunts said
(is it still true two and
a half decades later?)
"It don't mean nothing!"
All I know is, war is
not a metaphor for,
a style of,
or a symbol for,
life.
"Get your ass in the grass!,"
like the sergeant said,
And I have too,
write my own orders,
make my own meanings.

Horace Coleman holds an MFA from Bowling Green State University. In addition to being a former university professor, he has been a writer-in-the-schools, worked in public relations, been a technical writer, published in a number of anthologies and lived in six states. Originally from Ohio, he lives in Southern California. He is Vietnam War, "class of '67."